MW00815403

Acknowledgments

We'd like to express special thanks for our family and friends who've supported us through this journey.

Additionally, we couldn't have done this without all of the support from the amazing Quora Top Writers who we interviewed for this book.

Lastly, much love to the Quora community who started it all. We couldn't have done any of this without all of you.

Table of Contents

Introduction

If you are reading this book, chances are you are familiar with Quora. Maybe you were just like us and joined way back in the day when it first launched (circa 2009) and then promptly forgot about it.

It's only natural that over the past 5-6 years Twitter, Facebook, Pinterest and other platforms have completely taken over the spotlight.

Everyone else is talking about how to grow your Twitter following or how to run Facebook ads, but they are missing out on a MASSIVE opportunity.

In this book, we're going to break down all of the amazing benefits that Quora has provided in our personal and professional lives. We'll explain how we built our brands while making one-on-one connections with readers.

First off, let's tell you about our journeys using Quora...

Imran's Quora Journey

I started with Quora in 2009 when I simply opened up an account. I may have posted a question or two but nothing substantial.

I revisited it in June of 2015 after reading a post about one writer who had great success using it to build credibility while driving 10,000 visits and a ton of leads back to his blog. I've been hooked ever since.

I started like everyone else by just following topics I knew about or liked including Productivity, Passive Income, Self-Improvement, and a bunch of other ones.

I made it a point to answer at least 2-3 questions on a daily basis and have kept this habit up for the last few months. Slowly the views started rolling in. First 200, then 300, then up to 5000 views on some of my most indepth and best answers.

However, the results were slow.

I just didn't understand how some of the top writers would get 4-5 million views from only 100 answers or less!

What was I doing wrong?

I had already posted hundreds of answers. Most of them were really in-depth and high quality. I took hours creating them.

Then one day - my first big win.

I would like to generate relatively passive income of $500 per month through an online enterprise (e.g. a blog, affiliate marketing, etc.). I have about one year to do it. What should I do?

Re-Ask   Unfollow 110   Comment   Share   Downvote   ...

Imran's Answer

View 10 Other Answers

 Imran Esmail, I make coin writing & teaching people to write books
45.3k Views · Upvoted by Brandon Lee · Kemar Lawrence · 2 others you follow
Imran is a Most Viewed Writer in Passive Income.

$500 per month is not terribly difficult online - Here's what I would do to build up to $1000, $2000, $10,000 per month in "passive" income.

Step 1: Choose a Niche (2 weeks)
The biggest step is choosing a niche. This is sooooooooooooo important and where most people fail.

Because you NEED to choose something you actually care about or you won't be able to stick it out building the business.

You have to live, breathe and embody the type of person people want to be.

Upvoters 157   Comments 5   Share 1   ...

Just to clarify - from one post that took me 30 minutes to complete I got:

- 45,300 views

- 157 upvotes

- 5 comments

- 1 social media share

3

Apparently, Quora administrators thought my answer was good enough to feature it in the weekly digest that is emailed to 166,000+ subscribers.

This drove a ton of traffic back to my blog:

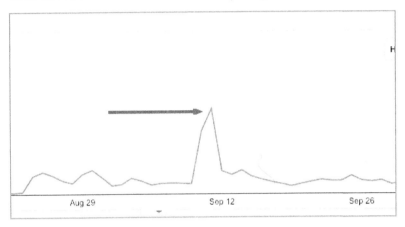

From that point I knew Quora had some real potential and I have continued to post answers on a daily basis.

Over these last few months, I've really come to enjoy the writing process and have met writers who I deeply respect like Dushka Zapata, Ellen Vrana and many others featured in this book.

Helping others, connecting with brilliant minds and my pure enjoyment of the writing process is what keeps me going.

Recently, I passed a significant milestone as well - I've now received 1,000,000 views across all my answers less than 6 months after I started writing on Quora!

Kevin's Quora Journey

Switching Careers

My first job out of college was in investment banking where I worked up to 100-120 hours per week. One of my most vivid memories is

Quora literally changed my entire life trajectory and helped me get to where I am today.

working on an M&A pitch for 2.5 days straight without sleep only to discover that I couldn't drive home because my car battery died, so I had to sleep under my desk for 3 hours and wake up in time to get materials printed for a client meeting.

Disclaimer: This photo isn't me. At least this guy had a jacket - I used styrofoam padding from a random fedex package as a blanket.

Since the investment bank I worked at blocked all forms of social media, I would use my phone any chance I got to browse Quora and keep myself sane.

One day, I was browsing Quora, and came across the topic of Product Management. I hadn't known much about the industry before but there was a huge community and plenty of questions and answers that taught me more about product management and advice on interviewing.

8 months into my investment banking job, I woke up and asked myself what I was doing with my life. **Using all of the information I learned from Quora,** I interviewed and somehow managed to receive a product manager offer.

The day I got my offer, I put my Blackberry and corporate credit card on my desk, walked into my staffer's office, and quit on the spot. On my way out, I took my favorite office painting off the wall, put it in my car trunk, and drove to San Francisco where I now live.

The painting that hangs on my apartment wall. Years later I finally told a VP who's still at the bank and we laugh about it every time we grab coffee.

Building My Brand and Launching My Website

After leaving the finance track to join a completely different industry, I decided to give back to the amazing Quorans who gave me so much advice when I was doing my own job search. I started writing for the product management topic and over time, people on Quora began to cold message or e-mail me to ask for advice on breaking into product management.

The feedback I was getting from people on Quora helped me realize that there was a **huge opportunity** to help people who had been in a similar position as me and I decided to start a website to teach people how to break into product management (www.productmanagerhq.com).

I continued writing on Quora and soon, Quora became my #1 traffic source - sending thousands of readers who became subscribers and helping to bring over 1000+ product managers from all over the world into my website's online Slack community.

Through my Quora answers, I've even had the chance to interact with some prominent product managers like Elynn Lee (Product Manager at Quora) and the CEO of Product School, Carlos González de Villaumbrosia, who found me through my Quora answers and invited me to become a regular instructor at his school; we're now great friends and frequently grab dinner together in the city.

I've even had moments where people at events in San Francisco have run up to me and told me they recognized me from my Quora answers online.

Bringing Me Back From My Darkest Moments

A year ago, I completely burned out from over-work and lost all of my motivation. I ended a 5.5 year relationship with my girlfriend and fell into a serious slump.

I almost quit everything.

I don't remember how, but somehow, I once again found myself back on Quora reading answers from people who had lost everything and pulled themselves back together. People like Leonard Kim, Brandon Lee, and James Altucher, whose answers and pure honesty brought me back to life. I internalized advice from writers like Dushka Zapata and Ellen Vrana.

I took one Quora writer's advice and began writing one post-it note every morning to motivate myself to never give up.

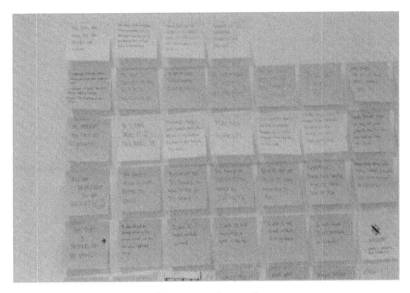

One corner of my wall.

And slowly, I brought myself back.

Living the Dream

So where has all of this led me?

After my past few years of ups and downs, I'm now a Product Manager at AltSchool, where I'm privileged to spend every day working on a mission to enable an exceptional and personalized education for every child in the world.

Through Quora, I've met amazing Top Writers like Brandon Lee, Nicolas Cole, Jordan Phoenix, and Charles Tips, some of whom I now consider great friends.

I'm literally living the dream and I couldn't have done any of it without Quora.

I've met my co-author Imran Esmail through a random Quora message and we managed to write this book and interview a dozen Quora Top Writers despite the fact that we live in different time zones and have never met in person.

For both of us, our success on Quora felt like dumb luck. We needed to figure out the formula that top writers were using to build their brands and get millions of views.

Breaking Down the Experts

We immediately went looking at the top experts on every topic. We had to answer questions like:

- What questions were they answering? And why?

- What was the composition of their answers? (Length, readability, etc.)

- Did they use images? Which ones and why?

- What tactics did they use to get you to click through to their website?

- How did they get people to follow them?

What You'll Learn

If you like Tim Ferriss, this is the book Tim Ferriss would have written if he were to break down how to master Quora.

What if you could get over 1,000,000 views in one day, featured on the front page of Reddit, and have major publications like Forbes, Inc., and Time magazine knocking down your door asking to publish your content?

Top Writers on Quora do this **ALL THE TIME...**

...and for the first time ever, we're going to share the secrets they use. We've interviewed over a dozen of Quora's best writers to understand:

- How a brand new writer got **129,000 views** on his answers within 24 hours

- How to dominate topics, become a prestigious Quora Top Writer, and get **exclusive access** to private Quora events

- How one Top Writer used Quora to **sell $1000 worth of books** within 24 hours of launch

- How another Top Writer got **published in major media** including Inc., TIME, Forbes, Fortune, The Huffington Post, Popsugar, Observer, Slate, and Business Insider

- How to include **calls to action** that get the reader so excited they MUST visit your website

- How to craft the **perfect profile** that gets thousands of views

- How top writers get their work published in a secret print book that Quora releases every year with a select few top answers

- and much more

Stop wasting hours writing content that no one ends up reading and get your writing in front of millions of people on Quora.

This is the book we wish we had before we started answering our first questions.

Enjoy,

Imran & Kevin

Why Bother with Quora

What is Quora? How did it start?

I f you're completely green coming into this book, Quora is a question and answer forum where a community of users ask, answer, edit and moderate discussion around every topic imaginable.

Quora was founded in 2009 by two former Facebook employees, Adam D'Angelo and Charlie Cheever. They were inspired to create Quora because:

> *"We thought that Q&A is one of those areas on the internet where there are a lot of sites, but no one had come along and built something that was really good yet."*

The Quora community by some estimates boasts 2.9 million active monthly users and has attracted big names like James Altucher, Marc Andreessen, Dustin Moskovitz, Jimmy Wales,

Stephen Fry, Ashton Kutcher, and Avicii who are regular contributors.

Even the President of the United States (https://www.quora.com/Whats-it-like-to-play-basketball-with-President-Obama/answer/Barack-Obama) has answered questions!

Now, let's talk about why we think it's worth your time over other social platforms...

Is it better than other social networks?

There are a lot of social networks out there. It's really difficult to figure out where to spend your time. Do you use Twitter, Facebook, Vine, YouTube, etc.?

There's just too much choice.

On the face of it, it doesn't seem like Quora would be a great use of your time:

Only a lowly 2.9 million monthly users as compared to Facebook's 1.49 billion.

However, we think that would be short-sighted because we've come to realize that **it's the quality of each interaction that matters** rather than the quantity of interactions.

Quora gives you plenty of opportunities to be memorable and make real quality connections with a lot of readers at once.

That's where the real strength of this platform lies.

Here are some interesting statistics on our new favorite social network:

- 9.1M Unique Visitors per Month according to Compete.com

- 145 Global Rank according to Alexa

- 24 Rank in India according to Alex

- 40% of visitors from India, 21% from United States according to Alexa

- 30% of visitors from search traffic according to Alexa

- Related sites: wikipedia, answers.com, reference.com, yahoo answers

- Five most followed topics for 2015: Technology (4.5M), Science (3.7M), Business (3.3M), Books (3.3M), Movies (2.9M)

- Monthly active users estimates - from 1.2M to 2.9M monthly active users

Who is it good for?

Quora is NOT for everyone.

If you're looking for a silver bullet or a quick way to get your content viral and build your brand, this isn't the book for you.

However, Quora IS great for:

–   Websites that rely on traffic for revenue (affiliate sites, content publishers, etc.)

–   Websites that sell informational products

–   Bloggers that want to establish themselves as an authority in their subject matter

–   Writers that want to build a loyal fanbase of readers and get published by major media

Long-form answers to direct questions from other human beings are a great way to show you KNOW what you are talking about and also convince people to check out your website and products.

Matan Shelomi (Quora Top Writer 2013, 2014, 2015)

https://www.quora.com/profile/Matan-Shelomi

"Quora is particularly suited for scientists. Several major funding agencies require grantees to share their findings with the greater community: to have "broader impacts."

One cannot get broader than the entire planet, so Quora is a perfect platform to spread information, especially since one's credentials and experience matter here. The objective truth matters here. Pseudoscience is downvoted here.

Quora users ask the questions on many people's minds, scientists write evidence-supported answers, and the media carries them to everyone else.

What better way to boost scientific literacy worldwide while establishing your reputation as an authority in your field?"

Now let's break down each of the pros and cons of using Quora.

The Pros and Cons

We've mentioned above why we've chosen Quora as our go-to resource for generating leads and building a brand, but let's dive deep into some of the pros and cons of using the service.

Not heavily used by internet marketers

Gary Vaynerchuk said, **"Internet marketers ruin everything."**

Well, it's true. As soon as they find a social media platform, they flood it with ads and figure out how to game the system.

Just look at Facebook or Instagram. **People are being driven away by advertisements.**

With Quora, there are no ways (as of yet) to show ads or pay for marketing. As a result, you are judged solely on the quality of your answers.

This levels the playing field for everyone.

Direct connection with people

Another thing Gary Vaynerchuk preaches is to **do the unscalable.**

By this, he means work your ass off to make those personal connections while everyone else floods people with links (ie. most marketers on Twitter) and useless information.

With questions on Quora, you know there is another person on the other end who is so desperate for an answer he couldn't find from Google that he has come to a Q&A platform.

Say Hi, be friendly and **you'll make a lasting impression with one person**. If your answer is really good and you're very charismatic, you can leave an impression on thousands of people.

People are doing it so wrong

Have a look through some of the answers on Quora and you'll notice (especially after reading this book) how poorly people are interacting on the platform.

It won't take you long to stand out from the pack using our techniques.

People often give answers that are criminally short; there is a lack of storytelling and use of images - things we will teach you in this book.

Your answer can get a ton of views in a short time

Check out this answer Imran left **only 5 days ago.**

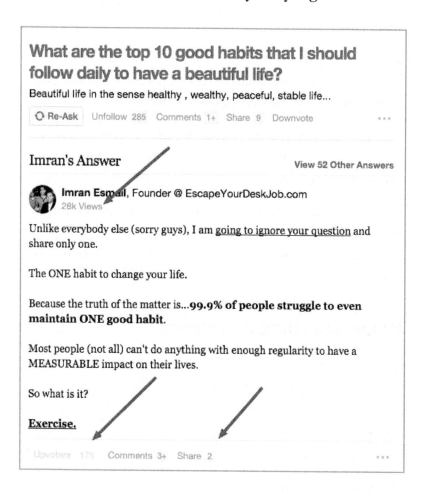

What are the top 10 good habits that I should follow daily to have a beautiful life?

Beautiful life in the sense healthy , wealthy, peaceful, stable life...

⟳ Re-Ask   Unfollow 285   Comments 1+   Share 9   Downvote   • • •

Imran's Answer   View 52 Other Answers

Imran Esmail, Founder @ EscapeYourDeskJob.com
28k Views

Unlike everybody else (sorry guys), I am going to ignore your question and share only one.

The ONE habit to change your life.

Because the truth of the matter is...**99.9% of people struggle to even maintain ONE good habit**.

Most people (not all) can't do anything with enough regularity to have a MEASURABLE impact on their lives.

So what is it?

Exercise.

Upvoters 175   Comments 3+   Share 2   • • •

28,000 views, 175 upvotes and 2 social shares.

This answer took him 20 minutes to write.

It all came down to good copywriting, a unique message and having some fun with it.

He quickly moved up to second or third in the rankings out of all the answers, and it will continue to sit there driving views to his profile and maybe to his website.

It's egalitarian

If you haven't guessed it already, anyone can post on Quora and all answers are treated as equal. Obviously, if you are a celebrity or expert in a field then your answer will receive more views and upvotes. Even if you aren't a celebrity, your answer stands right up there with others.

Quora is a level playing field, so if you are a newbie to internet marketing or don't know taxidermy, you can submit your two cents from what little you have learnt.

Every topic and niche is represented

Speaking of taxidermy - it's an open topic with 138 followers on Quora.

It just goes to show you that you can build a portfolio of answers on any topic. You can then later **use these posts to create a book or in content for your website.**

You can even brand yourself around a topic as Quora gives a badge for top writers on given topics.

Use this on your LinkedIn page, resume (maybe) and anywhere else you connect with people.

It's AMAZING for research into your target market

Before we realized how big an opportunity posting answers on Quora was, we used it almost exclusively for research into our target markets.

There are thousands of questions people have asked since 2009 all grouped into categories ready for you to pick out and answer in blog posts or in books.

We would (and still do) **turn these questions into sections of book** outlines.

Get answers from the experts

Did you know Avicii, Obama, and Ashton Kutcher to name a few have all posted answers on Quora at some point? If it's good enough for them, why aren't you on it yet?

Besides celebrities, there are a ton of experts from professors at Berkeley to astrophysicists at MIT. If you need an obscure question answered, this is the place to go.

You can get picked up by reputable media

Want to get published in Newsweek, Forbes, or Business Insider?

These publishers regularly mine Quora for good answers to re-publish on their platforms. Here's a sample of Google News search results:

About 130,000 results (0.32 seconds)

 Quora Question: What Was It Like to Be Black in the 196…
Newsweek - 6 hours ago
Quora Questions are part of a partnership between Newsweek and **Quora**, through which we'll be posting relevant and interesting answers …

 How Did Starbucks Initially Market The Pumpkin Spice Lat…
Forbes - Oct 16, 2015
This question originally appeared on **Quora.** Ask a question, get a great answer. Learn from experts and access insider knowledge. You can …

Delish

So, next time, instead of begging to be able to write for them, consider flipping the script and having them come to you!

Despite all of these great things, there are a few things to keep in mind before diving headlong into the world of Quora.

Good posts can take a long time

Don't kid yourself, a good answer takes time to think through and write up - sometimes as long as a blog post.

The good news is that if you invest your time correctly, it's much easier to get traffic and views on a Quora post than it is for a post on a new-ish blog.

Ain't no get rich quick scheme here.

Marketing is frowned upon

Finally, although not explicitly stated, marketing your own services or products is frowned upon.

Quora is first and foremost a service for you to help others. Shoving your product or service down people's throats will quickly show through and you'll get banned.

Instead, only answer questions you personally know and soft sell your services. We'll show you exactly how to do this later in the book.

That's it! Your pros and cons list.

Now read on through and find out what the experts do to stand out.

Deconstructing the Experts

The Perfect Topic Bio

Every time you leave an answer on any question, Quora will display about 50 characters including your name and your topic bio above your answer. Quora prompts you to have these topic-specific bios so that you can demonstrate expertise on the topic you're writing about. **Don't discount the importance of these 50 character bios!** When readers are scanning answers to a popular question, they'll check to make sure that your topic bio looks credible before deciding to invest their time in reading your answer.

In order to maximize the chance that your answers will get optimal view counts / upvotes / shares, take the first step of going to the right side of your public profile in the 'Knows About' section.

When you edit the section, you'll have the opportunity to add topics you know about as well as add short bios validating your topic expertise

For example, when I write answers to questions in the product management topic, I'll change my bio to demonstrate my experience in the field:

Kevin Lee, Founder @ Product Manager HQ, Product @ AltSchool, Prev. Product @ Kabam

Product Manager Interview: The Product Design Question ↗

One of the most important things I look for when interviewing potential candidates about product design is a framework or structure around their answers. If I ask a question around designing a product I expect the candidate to follow a structure such as the following:

1) Ask Clarifying Questions
Remember, there is no point continuing with an answer if you haven't fully grasped the situation. I can't count the number of times I've asked a simple product improvement question to a candidate who then proceeded to give me a lengthy 5 minute answer before I realized that the candidate had never used the product before. If I asked a candidate to walk me through how he/she might design a better wallet, I expect the candidate to first ask clarifying questions such as who the wallet might be used by, or what "better" means in

The Perfect Public Profile

Now that you've completed your topic bios, the next task is to craft the perfect public profile. Remember, spending the time to write lengthy answers or demonstrate topic expertise **means nothing** for your personal exposure if readers go to your profile and see nothing noteworthy or interesting.

Just like how all websites and businesses aim to convert visitors into subscribers or paying customers, your public profile is your chance to convert Quora readers into your followers and personal fans. I can't count the number of times I've had a follower message me on Quora telling me how they randomly came across my profile on Quora which led them to follow me, read all of my answers, and upvote / share them. I've even had Quora-celebrity moments where people approached me at events in San Francisco telling me that they recognized me from my Quora profile and from reading all my answers!

Before we go into a few case studies of perfect profiles, let's make sure you've got the basics covered. You should be filling out all information that Quora requests to include:

- About me section

- Areas of expertise

- Cities you belong in

- Schools / colleges you've attended

- Previous companies / work experience

- Other social media

All of this information adds extra visibility to your Quora profile. It also makes you more searchable when people are looking for specific Quora users to ask for answers. Additionally, Quora will sometimes do the work for you and send you notifications or e-mails asking you if you are able to answer a question simply because you've previously added topics of expertise.

Now let's take a look at two Quora Top Writers and how they've structured their perfect public profiles:

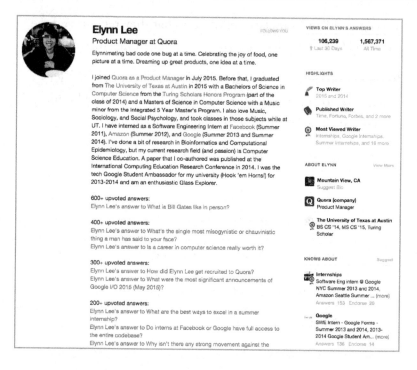

In this first example, we'll break down how Elynn Lee (https://www.quora.com/Elynn-Lee), a Product Manager at Quora, Published Writer, and Quora Top Writer in 2014/2015, effectively structures her Quora profile to further emphasize her expertise in the topics she writes for.

In her public profile, Elynn starts with a simple three sentence blurb to describe herself and to connect with her audience. You'll notice each sentence is intentional in its purpose:

Sentence 1: **[Career]** Describes a bit of her job responsibilities (with a pun to boot).

Sentence 2: **[Personal Interests]** Reveals an interest and love of food.

Sentence 3: **[Goals / Aspirations]** Describes what she enjoys thinking about.

Additionally, her three sentence blurb is cleverly short enough to feel personable to a reader and gives a glimpse into her life (a viewer can still see the blurb even if he/she doesn't click the 'more' button to expand her profile details).

In the detailed view of her profile, Elynn provides a longer paragraph that reveals her credentials and relevant work experience in the topics that she is a most viewed writer. She structures her detailed blurb in a way that appears academically rigorous as this helps reassure readers visiting her profile that she is a topic expert whose answers they can trust to be accurate.

Below her detailed blurb, she also conveniently provides links to her top upvoted answers separated by descending upvote count for easy reader access. One goal here with these links is to provide another gateway to her best answers and continues sending new cohorts of viewers / upvotes to help maintain these answers' top positions in their respective topics.

In this second example, Nicolas Cole (https://www.quora.com/Nicolas-Cole-1), a writer / fitness model / entrepreneur, Published Writer, and Top Writer of 2015, takes a different approach in using his Quora profile to help build his personal brand.

Nicolas chooses to start his public profile with a **captivating one-liner** that encourages a reader to want to learn more about his story. If his one-liner isn't enough to capture your attention, he then immediately follows up with a **list of credible media sources** that he's been published in to help build legitimacy. Here, we see that Nicolas has intentionally left out a detailed blurb about his life story, potentially so that the reader questions what is so fascinating about his story that led to him being published.

Nicolas then takes an opportunity to add outbound links to promote his personal website, link to his published workout routine / nutrition guide books, and encourages readers to sign up to be part of a mailing list for his upcoming book.

He also links to his most popular answers that define his personal story and takes a last opportunity to guide readers towards following his other social media such as Facebook, Twitter, and Instagram. Through his public profile, we can see how Nicolas is a prime example of a Quora Top Writer who effectively leverages Quora to build his personal brand both on and off the platform.

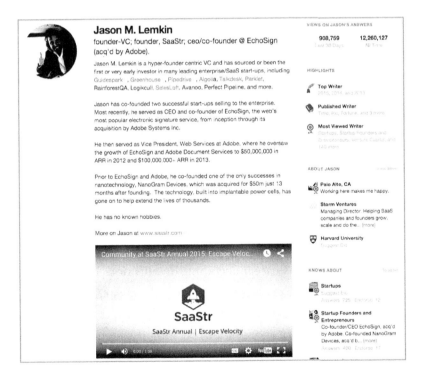

In this last example, Jason M. Lemkin (https://www.quora.com/Jason-M.-Lemkin), a serial entrepreneur / VC, Published Writer, and Top Writer of 2013/2014/2015, takes a straightforward approach of laying out his personal career successes to validate his expertise.

To help accentuate his expertise in topics like Startups and Venture Capital, Jason breaks out the paragraphs in his detailed profile to call out accomplishments in different stages of his career. His first paragraph outlines his experience as a VC investor while listing his numerous individual startup investments. To avoid being labeled a VC with no operating experience, he then follows up with three paragraphs demonstrating his experience as a founder of successfully acquired startups. Furthermore, he seeks to build goodwill with readers by using the example of one of his first companies, NanoGram Devices, to show how he has helped extend the lives of thousands. In Top Writer fashion, he ends in a strong finish with a humorous message by noting that "he has no known hobbies."

One thing to note here is that Jason treats his profile much like a business would, in using free content or content marketing to build trust with a potential customer before pitching them on purchasing a product. Only after Jason has guided a reader through his profile's career accomplishments does he take the opportunity to link readers to his external website/blog SaaStr. Additionally, he effectively links a video for SaaStr in case a reader wants to learn more before clicking through the external link.

Attributes of a Perfect Answer

Quora's mission is to create the best page on the internet for any given question. In order to do that, readers need to consider these pages as concise, valuable and credible.

High quality answers should be helpful for the direct poster of the question as well as anyone around the world who might have the same question. Specifically, Quora has outlined that a perfect answer should have some of the following attributes:

Addresses the question that was asked.

A perfect answer should follow the subject and consider the frame of mind of the person asking the question - i.e., what they are thinking about, what they need clarity on, and what context should be provided.

Provides content that is reusable for anyone who has the same question.

A perfect answer contains facts and insight that are relevant and reusable. Providing facts helps ensure that the answer you provide isn't customized just to one specific person. If you plan on providing personal anecdotes or opinions, then you need to provide the appropriate context to support the case for your point of view. Perfect answers are able to cover multiple-use cases with various conditions (i.e., "If your tax bracket is X amount, you should invest using Y method") so that more readers can relate to your answer.

Be credible and include accurate facts.

A perfect answer should be able to convince a reader that it's accurate and trustworthy. You should be double checking all of your facts to ensure that nothing is misleading or incorrect or else you'll damage your reputation for that answer and any future answers. (The Quora audience is meticulous and highly intelligent!) Many of the perfect answers that we've seen have included a list of referenced sources at the end of the answer. Additionally, you should be indicating why you are qualified to provide a credible answer.

Tony Stubblebine (Quora Top Writer 2014)

https://www.quora.com/profile/Tony-Stubblebine

"I only play to win. Partly that's moral - why steal someone else's shine if they are doing a great job? And partly it's practical. A top answer can generate traffic for years.

For example, there were several meditation questions that I went after. The existing answers were all solid personal anecdotes. But I happened to have data from helping 95,000 people start meditation practices.

So I put together several very lengthy answers complete with charts and graphs. Then I made sure to recruit enough people to upvote my answers into the top spot. Those answers have now driven more than two years of traffic.

If I don't think I can win the answer then I'll skip it."

Stay concise and easy to read.

Perfect answers are very easy for someone to read, even if they are quickly glancing or skimming through multiple answers on a page. Many top writers will oftentimes break up their answers into structured formats with simple formatting (i.e., bullets, lists, bolded header sections). Make sure you run your answer through a spell check and read it aloud to verify that the grammar and punctuation are correct.

What Top Writers Say About Perfect Answers

In addition to the tips that Quora has laid out for composing high quality answers, we synced up with some of Quora's most popular writers to get their advice on how to write perfect answers that have generated hundreds of thousands of views.

Top writers recommend that you should:

Appropriately include humor

Perfect answers that garner a critical mass of views and upvotes will appropriately add humor. A prime example of this is Sander Daniels' (Thumbtack Co-Founder, Most Viewed Quora Writer) answer to the Quora question: "What is it like to work at a startup that's on fire?" (Source: https://www.quora.com/What-is-it-like-to-work-at-a-startup-thats-on-fire) See his humorous answer that has garnered 206,000 views and 5,200 upvotes below:

"Imagine this:

Since you were 7 years old, you had your eye on marrying the most beautiful, kindest girl in the entire world, Julie Dream.

However, you were the ugliest and shortest person in school. Nobody knew your name. Everyone ignored you. You were nobody.

In middle school you formed an action plan to get this girl. This was the brainstorming phase of your pursuit. You had lots of crazy ideas. Maybe you should buy a Super Bowl ad to get her attention. Maybe you should borrow millions of dollars and hire a PR firm to get your name out around school. Maybe you should invest all your resources in an inbound marketing campaign, building out your personal blog, becoming a guest columnist in your school newspaper, or creating infographics about how awesome you are. Maybe people would link to your infographic when discussing the concept of 'awesomeness' generally.

None of these things, however, promised immediate return. These things all seemed tangential to achieving the dream.

In high school you decided on an action plan. From here on out, you were going to take concrete action to make your dream come true. You were going to lift weights. You were going to read books and get smart. You were going to get the best grades. You were going to take lessons on how to be funny and how to dance well.

In short, you were going to do everything you could for however long it took to get this girl, and you thought about it every waking moment of your life. And that's what you did.

In college, the rubber hit the road. It was time to get serious. Julie still didn't know your name, and you weren't getting any traction towards even dating her. However, you saw faint indications that your plan had worked for others, so if you worked hard enough and dreamed big enough, it might actually work for you. Some of your older friends had grown up and gotten their dream girls with similar techniques. Julie was still eluding you, but somehow she felt nearer than a few years ago.

You tripled the time spent in the gym, the time you spent studying, the time you spent learning how to be cool. Your Body Mass Index was plummeting. Someone told you Julie had mentioned you in conversation at a party. It seemed like you had kind of figured out a formula that might be working. You stepped on the accelerator; you didn't sleep.

College was nearing an end, though, and you felt like you were reaching a decision point. Although some indicators looked great, some didn't look so great.

For example, in addition to having an awesome body and personality that your girl didn't even notice, you were ditching other great opportunities in pursuit of this girl. Your parents thought Julie Dream was in the "fast group" - too risky and volatile to attain. They wished you would just settle down with the ones who were actively courting you - Gail Goldman & Sarah Sachs.

Meanwhile, Julie was dating lots of other guys you looked up to on campus - Gary Google, Frank Facebook, and Tony Twitter. These guys were all 10 years older than you. These were beefy dudes, Big Men on Campus, and could provide any lady with more security than you ever could.

The worst thing was that Gary, Frank and Tony even seemed to be encroaching on your space. Every good idea you had for getting Julie - they did something similar. Every wing-man you tried to recruit to your cause - they recruited with greater ease. These guys had already achieved the dream - were they trying to shut the door behind them?

You made a decision to ignore Gail & Sarah - those seductive ladies who wanted you so bad they actually paid for your dinner. You also decided to ignore Gary, Frank and Tony - your worries wouldn't change anything they might do in pursuit of their dream. It took superhuman willpower to keep your eye on your dream, ignore all the best advice of your family and friends, and forge on.

You graduated from college, and finally... you started seeing some real traction. At this point, your body was stunningly chiseled. Your mind was brilliant. You were hilarious.

You were better in every way than all of Julie's incumbent contenders.

Your big break came when you got noticed by Julie's three best friends - Sandra Sequoia, Katie Kleiner, and Allison Andreessen. Not only did they notice you - they all started pursuing you, all at the same time, without any warning. You were suddenly the hottest thing in town. These three people had never heard of you two months ago, and now they all wanted your sexy body. And they were fighting over it. And the world was noticing.

These girls did so many ridiculous things to secure you as a long-term fling that Techcrunch, Shamable, and OmGiga - the three most popular gossip blogs on campus - didn't stop coverage of this insane bidding war for weeks on end.

And even though you knew that getting into a relationship with one of Julie's best friends could take over your life and meddle with your dream, you did it anyway - because you had seen others do it before you and they seemed like the fastest way to getting Julie, who you have dreamed of every moment of every day since you were 7 years old.

So here you are. You are living the dream that 99.99% of people in the world would kill for - you are super-buff, super-smart, super-funny, generally respected by your small campus community as super-awesome... and you're dating one of the hottest girls around. Taken together, life is good.

But you want more.

You're thrilled you've made it this far, but what you have isn't enough. Your middle school plan is working great, but you still doubt and question it. You're having fun and you love the pursuit, but you just don't know whether you'll ever get Julie Dream.

That's what it's like to work at a start-up that's on fire."

Remember, there is plenty of evidence to show that readers will upvote and share content that makes them laugh much more often than content that simply makes them go "hmm" and ponder the answer.

Add relevant images / video

One way top writers clearly differentiate their perfect answers amongst a sea of text is by including relevant images / video that can help capture a reader's attention. One example of a great answer that has extremely relevant images is Subhrajyoti Ghatak's answer to the Quora question: "What are the most gripping stories in human history?" (Source: https://www. quora.com/What-are-the-most-gripping-stories-in-human-history/answer/Subhrajyoti-Ghatak) See his answer that has garnered 280,000 views and 6,400 upvotes below:

"This is a story, which will not be there in the pages of any important history book. This is a story too local for a globalized world. Here is a hero driven by far more mundane issue such as access to a doctor, rather than desire to build an empire.

This is the story of **Dashrath Majhi**

Dashrath Majhi's *wife died without any treatment, because the nearest town with a Doctor was 70 km away from their village in Bihar, India. Well that could have been a far shorter distance, if not for a hill in between the village and the town.*

Dashrath *did not want anyone else to suffer the same fate as his wife. So he did the unthinkable:*

From Wikipedia:

Dashrath Manjhi's *claim to fame has been the herculean task of single-handedly carving a 360-foot-long (110 m), 25-foot-high (7.6 m) and 30-foot-wide (9.1 m) road by cutting a mountain of Gehlour hills with a hammer, chisel and nails working day and night for 22 years from 1960 to 1982. This passage reduced the distance between Atri and Wazirganj blocks of Gaya district from 70 km to just 7 km.*

Here is the man

And here is the mountain he cleaved **alone.**

Link to other answers and people

By using the "@" symbol, you can link or copy the URL of a previous answer you've already given or tag other Quora writers/readers who you think could benefit from the answer. If you are active about building your Quora network, tagging others can help provide extra attention to your answer if they share your answer with their own followers or simply help provide edits / advice to make your answer even better.

Finish strong

Like a good speech or presentation, a perfect answer should end on a high note or provide a great summary. Perhaps you might even want to end with a humorous note or joke. Some top writers believe that a strong anecdote, picture, or take-away can make a reader feel rewarded for reading your entire answer.

More tips from the experts

Dushka Zapata (Quora Published Writer - Inc., The Huffington Post, Thought Catalog)

https://www.quora.com/profile/Dushka-Zapata

"To me, the secret of a good answer lies in the question.

There are three types of questions:

- *The ones I can't answer because I don't know. (Such as - what does it feel like to walk on the moon?)*

- *The ones I could answer but am not personally fascinated by. (What is the world's fastest car?)*

- *The ones that I read and they tug at my heart so strongly I would get out of bed in the middle of the night to answer them. (I'm blind. What does it feel like to see?)*

If you answer what yanks at your heart, it's more likely that what you write will have that effect on your readers."

Bala Senthil Kumar (Quora Top Writer 2014/2015)

https://www.quora.com/profile/Bala-Senthil-Kumar

"The perfect answer is one that informs and inspires, tantalizes and provokes, opens doors to worlds we may not know much about, and leaves us thirsty for more.

It does not look for approval, validation or appreciation, and is usually written by a gloriously imperfect person with a view on life far different from our own and many miles on a journey unknown to the rest of us."

Dominating on Quora - The Play-by-Play

As we mentioned before, there is no silver bullet or magic formula that's going to get your content viral, immediately build your brand, or quickly get you noticed by major media. But we've interviewed over a dozen Quora Top Writers and here are some of the strategies they use that can significantly increase your chances:

Pay someone to find the top posts in your niche

We only have so much time to spend working on Quora answers. We'd rather spend the majority of our time crafting amazing answers to questions that people are actually following.

In that vein, we recommend outsourcing as much of the research process as possible so that when you login, you can get right into answering the right questions.

Here's the system we use to make our time on Quora more efficient:

Quora doesn't give you an easy way to find the most followed questions on your topic.

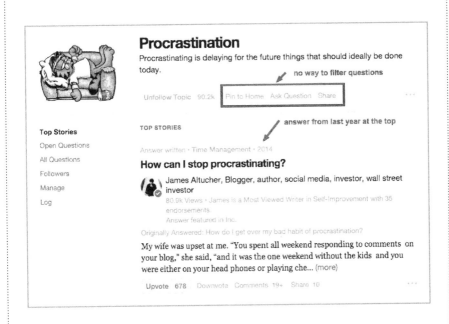

You will have to do this yourself.

If you remember, we mentioned that choosing hot questions with lots of followers is a surefire way to get a lot more views in a short amount of time.

So, what you can do, is hire a virtual assistant on OnlineJobs.ph or Fiverr.com and give them access to your account.

Obviously you don't want to share your password, so we use Lastpass.com to manage our passwords and share them with others https://helpdesk.lastpass.com/sharing/ without them knowing the password.

Next, have them go through the topics you want and add the top followed question (think in the range of 500+ followers and 100K views or more on a question) to your answer later list.

When you login next, you will be able to quickly jump to this list and start answering the top questions! It **should only cost $10-15 for an hour's worth of research** and it's worth the investment.

Of course, you could do this yourself but either way, having a lineup of questions to answer each day makes our writing process much more fluid.

Start with a snappy headline

Oliver Emberton, one of Quora's most successful writers with over 9 million views, commonly states during interviews that one of the most important ways he grabs attention instantly is to start with a snappy opening hook. You can usually tell from an opening paragraph whether the answer is going to be successful or not and good writing is able to capture your attention with the very first sentence.

How can I stop procrastinating?

○ Re-Ask   Follow 14.6k   Comments 3   Share 3   Downvote   ⋯

Oliver's Answer   View 1934 Other Answers

 Oliver Emberton, read and lived over 200 self-improvement books
1.1m Views • Upvoted by Alecia Li Morgan • Elynn Lee • 3 others you follow
Answer featured in Time and 1 more.
Oliver has 53 endorsements in Self-Improvement.
Originally Answered: How do I get over my bad habit of procrastination?

I'll answer your question, but first I need to explain all of human civilisation in 2 minutes with the aid of a cartoon snake.

Humans like to think we're a clever lot. Yet those magnificent, mighty brains that allow us to split the atom and touch the moon *are the same stupid brains that can't start an assignment until the day before it's due.*

Answer one question in detail every day

You don't need many GOOD answers to stand out on Quora. So, **stick to a schedule**. We typically **answer one or two**

questions per day and are able to get 20,000+ views on any given answer once in awhile.

Use your budget to spend money on illustrations and other graphics to enhance your answers. Again, you can find someone to work on these images on Fiverr.

Post relevant links for more information

If you want to drive quality, relevant traffic back to your website then add relevant links below your answer.

These links can be to your social profiles or to your website. Make sure you make it intriguing enough that the reader wants to find out more.

Maybe this is bonus material they can download, expanded details on the question you just answered, email courses or anything you can give to make them take action.

Add in Rich Media - optional (SlideShares, Videos, Images, etc.)

Finally, after you have written your answer, add in media to make it really stand out.

We don't recommend doing this while you're writing, because **the message is more important than the support material.**

We typically leave it until the end and find relevant stuff on the web to add in. Videos are the best because they make your answer stand out and people love watching film.

Add Your Business + Post Questions

Have you added your business as a topic on Quora yet?

Did you even know you can? This is how it looks:

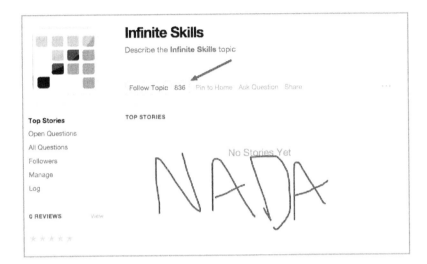

This is a random page Imran found which appears to be for a company (hence the logo). You can see they have more than **800 followers but have asked zero questions on the topic.**

Opportunity missed...

Now this is cool for a few reasons:

- **People can follow your business** and will be notified when questions or answers come up around the topic. While most people don't build a following on Quora, you can and will stand out.

- **You can ask questions about your business** or on a topic related to your business and tag your business in the question. This can get people to notice your business especially if the question gains traction. Tip: Ask the question anonymously, so it doesn't seem like you're gaming the system.

- **You can ask people to answer your question about your business** or on a related topic. This will bring new people into the fold who will learn about your activities.

Answer questions in trending topics

TRENDING NOW

- The Walking Dead Season 6 Episode 1

- Dell to Buy EMC

- The Martian

- CNN Democratic Primary Debate

If you look below your feed after logging in, you should see a section that says "Trending Now."

Of course, these topics change every day, but keep an eye on them and see if a topic pops up that you could provide a good answer for.

The top writers on Quora can be seen hanging out on it because they know they can rack up the views in the short amount of time by answering a question or two.

Here's Robert Frost:

Answer written · ↗ The Martian (2015 movie) · Mon

Why didn't they use cryo sleep technology in the film "The Martian", which would have given the survivor more sol to survive?

Robert Frost, Read it. Seen it.
18k Views · Upvoted by Marc Bodnick, seen 2000+ movies · Konstantinos Konstantinides, Electrical Engineer and Patent Agent
Robert is a Most Viewed Writer in The Martian (2015 movie).

Maybe because cryo-sleep technology doesn't exist. If it did exist, why would there be a cryogenic sleep machine on the Martian surface? Maybe because it would have been a &@$*#%* boring book and... (more)

Upvote 515   Downvote   Comments 9+   Share

Notice the views and the date - **that was only three days ago, and he has already racked up** 18,000 views and 515 upvotes.

Here's another one by him:

Another one with **62.9K views and another 2,600 upvotes** posted one day before the last one. He quickly became the top writer for the movie.

While you may not be an expert on every topic, with a little research and a good post, you can quickly climb up the rankings and get seen by a lot of people.

This will help towards being noticed as a top writer on Quora and, hopefully, you can pick up a bunch of followers and people who check out your profile.

Asking the right questions

Although we spent a lot of time focusing on the importance of writing answers, asking the right questions can be just as important. Sometimes, you can become a leader in a niche simply by asking great questions and being noticed by people following the topic.

One way to start is by looking at following top writers within a topic and seeing what kinds of questions they are asking that receive a high amount of views or answers. Additionally, as you ask questions, you can also target specific writers using the Ask to Answer feature.

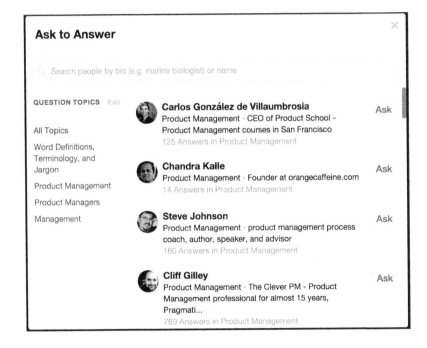

Since asking someone to answer a question shoots them an e-mail as well as a Quora notification, this is much more likely to get you on their radar if they are potentially influential for you or your business.

Sometimes companies will intentionally ask questions to get a sense of which topics their customers are more curious or confused about. Asking these questions can help them generate sales leads as they can gather information on people who've answered, commented, shared, upvoted, or generally engaged with the question. If you run a blog or work in the media industry, you can ask questions to crowdsource article content or article topic ideas.

Bright RED profile image

One interesting way one writer drew attention to his profile picture was by making it a bright color.

Check out what Ryan Stewart - a guy who drives tons of monthly views from Quora - did:

Now when he went to answer a question, his answer would stick out like a sore thumb:

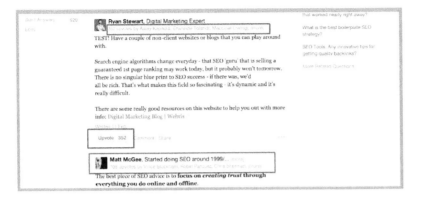

Whatever you can do to make your profile stand out, take the opportunity to separate yourself from everyone else out there.

Mention other writers in your answer

When we post, we quickly read through the other answers on the question.

If we like one, we mention the writer right at the top:

Johnny FD: $7,646.28 in Profits for Sept 2015

Sam Priestley can probably weigh in on his Table Tennis Sleeve.

I think he said he's pulling in $10,000 per month - Step-By-Step Guide to Creating and Selling a Physical Product

Its a great business after you put everything in place. The upfront work is the challenge and where most people stall.

Anyways, we do books - but my next project may be drop-shipping.

Good luck!

Written 3h ago

Upvoters 0   Comment   Share   . . .

The other writer will get a notification similar to this one:

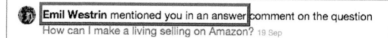

Emil Westrin mentioned you in an answer comment on the question How can I make a living selling on Amazon? 19 Sep

Emil Westrin commented on your answer to How can I make a living selling on Amazon? 19 Sep
A fantastic blog post Imran Esmail! Thanks for sharing.
Reply

This is great for a few reasons:

- It **gets you on the radar of other writers,** which is awesome if you want to later do business with this person or get advice from them.

- They appreciate the vote of confidence. **It's more powerful than an upvote** because you are acknowledging them right at the beginning of your answer.

It's really simple as well...just type an "@" symbol and a list of names will appear. Then start typing the person or topic you want to reference.

Here's a screenshot:

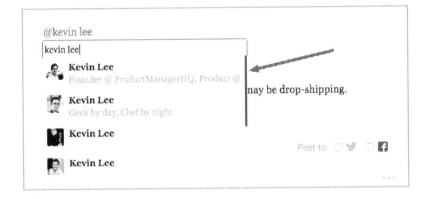

Dominate 2-3 categories

When you first start out, it can be tempting to choose a dozen categories and start answering questions in all of them at once.

Here's the problem:

- **You never get known for anything.** Want a badge next to your name to show you are a top writer? Then you need to focus on one or two topics and stand out.

- **You don't get as many A2A.** Usually, the people that are getting asked to answer questions are those same top writers. If you want people to see you as a leader and ask you questions, then focus.

Don't worry though because what ends up happening is you will **automatically get ranked for other related topics** because the questions you answer have multiple tags on them.

Make Your First 3 Lines Controversial

In the notification bar, people who are following a question will get a notification on any new answers for the question.

Typically, the notification only shows the first three lines (see below) and if the three lines are interesting enough, they will be enticed to look into your answer.

 Vandana Yadav wrote an answer to What are the top 10 good habits that I should follow daily to have a beautiful life? 11h ago
10 upvotes by Archana Asok Nair, Ravinder Ravi, (more)

1 Early to bed,early to rise:
First thing to start a good day is to wake up early and have a glass of warm water. According to researchers warm water cleans up stomach and ...

Unfollow

The point is, like a blog post or tweet or any form of communication, it's important to **hit off with your most intriguing comments to get people's attention.**

Use Images

Whenever we can, we include an image from Giphy.com or elsewhere. You can find an image on any topic and it really adds to your answer.

People are visual afterall.

Here's one example:

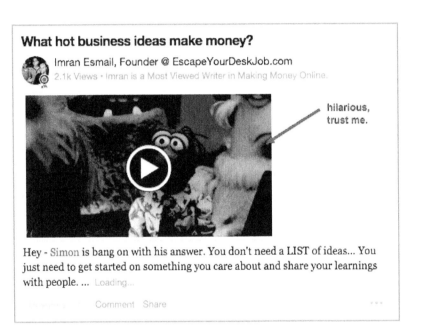

Images are a great way to spice up your answer just don't overdo it. **Make sure the images are relevant to the content you are writing.** The optimal image placement is every 75 to 100 words according to Buzzsumo.

From the horse's mouth:

It's shown to double the amount of shares vs. articles with fewer images, and a minimum of 30 more shares than articles with more images - Buzzsumo Genius

Track Clicks in Google Analytics

Most people forget to track clicks to their website within Google Analytics. This will go a long way to show you that your efforts writing these long posts are paying off.

Here's how we do it:

Step 1: Install Google Url Builder for Chrome or Firefox

Step 2: Click the plug-in on the page you want to share

When you want to share a page from your website, click the plugin and fill in all the details. The most important part is to put "source" as "quora" and "medium" as "post." These are UTM parameters.

You can even put in details of what question you have answered to differentiate between answers, but we don't bother.

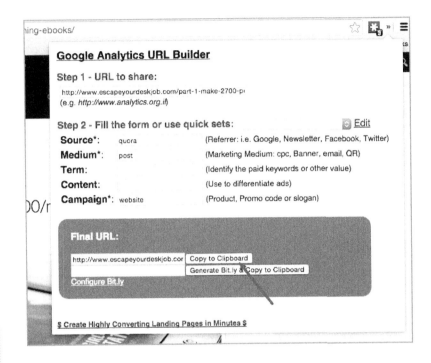

Step 3: Paste the link in your Quora answer

Next, paste the link that's generated into your Quora answer. You can even edit it to make it read how you want. See below:

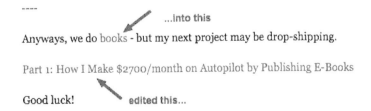

Step 4: Watch your Google Analytics

Finally, monitor your Google analytics for the results of your efforts.

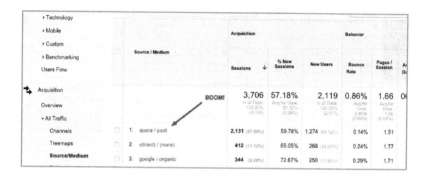

Bonus!

Want to get on the radar of big bloggers?

Try adding your Twitter handle or a memorable one-liner to those UTM parameters when linking to other blogs.

They will surely check their analytics and maybe get back to you.

Interviews with Top Writers

INTERVIEW WITH BRANDON LEE

Entrepreneur, Real Estate Investor, TEDx Speaker

Quora Profile (https://www.quora.com/profile/Brandon-Lee-11): Quora Top Writer 2015, Published Writer (Time, Inc., BBC, Mashable), Most Viewed Writer in 14 Topics

Getting Started

How and when did you get started writing on Quora?

July 4, 2014. I had been reading James Alchuter's writing for two weeks straight and I came across his post on What is James Alchuter's Secret for Blogging so Consistently. In his opening line, he said he had been writing for 24 years. Every day for 24 years, he would spend 2-4 hours of his morning reading, and then 2-4 hours on writing. That was a light bulb moment where I said, **"I gotta start somewhere."**

Clearly, his style of writing and ability to write was a byproduct of 24 years of practice. I commented on that answer two weeks later saying, "I just recently started a similar habit. Forcing myself just to write 100-200 words a day seems a lot more feasible than the daunting task of 'write two hours a day' or 'write a novel.'"

So I actually started based on that premise. I started writing a few hundred words every day. Initially, I started writing on Evernote but ran out of topic ideas so I started writing on Quora.

What led you to keep writing?

It was that commitment, **purely that commitment** of writing 200-300 words per day. That was the only reason. At that point I know it was the sheer practice of writing that kept me going. I used to run my own blog anyway, so I've had experience writing.

Starting out, my original misconception was that my content wasn't that good. I thought that other people were already writing about the exact same topics I was writing in, so I didn't think there was a space I could carve out. But I just started writing anyway. I wrote answers I thought that I deeply understood and stuck with topics that I knew.

Sometimes I looked at answers that just totally sucked and thought to myself, "OK, I can totally write a better answer than this." It was a mix, I tried to never write with an intention; I had to just get better at writing and wanted to keep **exercising my writing muscles.**

Finding your Niche

When you kept writing, did you try to find topics that had the most following? Within these topics, did you try to target specific questions?

Well, it just so happened and wasn't so much of an effort, that self-improvement is one of the **most followed** topics, so it just worked. I stuck on a few things and there just happened to be a lot of viewership. I wrote in niche topics, too, like mentorship just because I wanted to write about it and see what other people were writing about.

I never initially tried to find answers that might get the most views. I literally just browsed. Additionally, I had been following top writers like Leonard Kim (Quora Top Writer 2014/2015) at the time, and he wrote about the same stuff. Sometimes I would write answers to the same questions he answered, because I felt like I had a legitimate answer to supplement it.

Again, I rarely tried to "find" specific questions. At that point, I was already using Quora 3-4 hours a day anyway.

Do you actively track your follower count?

I used to keep track of my follower count for the first eight months. I actually have an excel spreadsheet of how many followers I was getting per month haha. Leonard Kim started maintaining it and wrote about it in one of his answers. So I thought to myself, "You know, I think I should probably keep a spreadsheet myself to show that I'm improving as a writer."

Crafting Your Answers

Have you tried to establish a concrete structure to your answers to maximize upvotes / views?

Formatting is a big deal for a lot of people. Personally, I'm not a fan of the list format... but I **KNOW IT WORKS**. So I only do it when I feel there's like there's a flow that makes sense for me to follow the list format.

Otherwise, I'm just using my own line of thinking. I have my own process of how I write, and I try to stay true to that versus using a list format. I personally don't feel like it's a quality format for good quality or showing depth.

How do you feel about using images within your answers?

Images definitely work, but admittedly, sometimes it can feel like clickbait haha. When you're browsing through a bunch of answers, of course an image will stand out. 90% of my answers don't have photos, mainly because I'm lazy and I'm not actively aiming to get views.

I just want to write good content. Maybe that's bad marketing, but I started on Quora to be a better writer and get good content out there.

The Top Writer Experience

As a Top Writer, do you have a great relationship with other writers?

I try to talk to a handful of other Top Writers. I probably know Charles Tips (Quora Top Writer 2015) the best out of every other Top Writer. I talk to Leonard Kim the most though. I'll also chat with Nicolas Cole (Quora Top Writer 2015) and Mike Xie (Quora Top Writer 2014/2015). These are probably the four main Top Writers I maintain contact with. I've had some great conversations with a few others like Ellen Vrana, Mike Leary, and Mira Zaslove as well; everyone who is a Top Writer definitely has an interesting story, though some are more sociable than others in person.

What was the experience like when you became a Quora Top Writer? Were there any perks / opportunities?

One of the best parts of becoming a Quora Top Writer is the **camaraderie** and **level of respect** that comes with it.

When I first started writing, I mentioned Leonard in my answers, because I knew it was a tactic to get his attention, but I was also legitimately trying to acknowledge his answers. And I know we are all biased in our generalizations, so he probably just thought of me as another fan.

But I just kept writing, and right around when I got a message from Quora staff saying I was being nominated for a Top Writer, I started to really refine my content. Leonard started following me a bit more and there was this psychological aspect where he may have thought "OK, this guy's actually pretty legit." So being a Top Writer gets you a certain level of respect from people and **definitely opens doors to talk to other Top Writers**.

You also get free Quora T-shirts at the meetups haha. These meetups happen every 6 months (generally May / November) and I've attended every single one I've been invited to. Most Quora Top Writers are also in the Quora Anthology. Quora 2014 Anthology was a book where they published one top answer from every Top Writer, so it was an actual book series. It's actually a pretty useful book and it's limited edition; you can't buy it anywhere, so I guess that was pretty cool.

Do you think being a Top Writer has benefited you outside of the platform? With your own brand?

Absolutely, especially in the various business communities I'm a part of. Most entrepreneurs are aware of Quora. So I can say, as a Top Writer, I have X Million views which causes them to think "OK, this guy is legit."

I have written before and know that dynamic of people having this preconceived notion of who you are after seeing your work online. They box you into who they want you to be and if they are a fan, they tend to not give you permission to be someone else in their mind. This is why I'm friends with other Top Writers because I know how to treat them like normal people and still have healthy respect for what each other has done. I try as little as possible to not drop the title of Top Writer because I don't like being put on a pedestal. It's fun the first few times when you aren't used to the attention, but once you've been there, it's not as enticing.

When Quora notified you they were nominating you to be a Quora Top Writer, how did that process work?

There doesn't seem to be a formal process. There is one guy, Jonathan Brill, Writer Relations at Quora, who manages relationships with Top Writers. He has a funnel of people notifying him of Quora writers he might want to check out.

Becoming a Quora Top Writer seems to be a mixture of either having expertise in a unique topic or having legitimate content that gets a lot of views / gets published - it could also be some combination of those. So again, no formal process, but Jonathan messaged me one day saying something along the lines of, *"Hey, I like your answers and I'm thinking of putting you in our next class of Quora Top Writers."*

What's the process of getting published in major media?

Someone on Quora's staff will definitely ask first. They'll say, *"We're considering this piece for this publication, are you cool with it?"* Then they'll send me the final article. So all in all, it's pretty straightforward and they generally contact me through Quora as well.

Next Level Tips

Would you say there's any next level tips you've discovered that other Quora writers might not be doing?

"Tactically, you should have **concise thoughts.** *Have an opinion and know how to convey it. Use* **analogies, good storytelling,** *and* **know how to evoke emotion** *in your answers. Tactically if you can do all those things, you'll naturally already have good formatting in your answers.*

Strategically, you just need to **have opinions or answers that most other people don't have or think about** *that make sense and are coherent. And I think this is the bigger challenge. Even if you are tactical in your answers, it doesn't matter if you don't have good ideas or don't know how to convey them.* **So strategically, have a unique opinion that people believe is worth following."**

For me, a lot of my writing is actually just a byproduct of actual real-life conversations that I've had. **Most of the stuff I write was field-tested in conversation.** It was tested in an mentorship or advisory relationship and I transferred it to writing. So I know from testing that my writing will generate results. But I think for most budding writers, they tend to think their writing is the most unique thing on the planet, but they haven't tested it in real-life conversation so they actually don't have any idea if their content is worthwhile or not.

> "All-in-all, it's just so cool that Quora is this **validation ground** where people can follow or upvote you. It's honestly a reflection of your writing. **If people don't click follow after you write, that's real feedback."**

There are people who write hundreds of answers and only have a few followers. And this is probably because their quality of writing isn't that good! For me, **studying other top writers and highly upvoted answers** was pretty important from the get-go. I'd think to myself "How did this answer get thousands votes?" improve my own answers, and get better that way.

Any last next-level tips?

The biggest key is just consistency. Starting out, I wrote three answers a day for three months straight. Right now, I'm still averaging 5000 views a day but I only write 3-4 answers a month now.

So in the beginning, it's like building a blog; people are going to want legit consistent content. At the beginning, there's a direct correlation with your writing and your follower count. **After you hit 2000-3000 followers, then you have a critical mass and people will naturally just follow you regardless of your writing.** So again, consistency is important.

I think for the first 30 days, I never had an answer that had more than 17 upvotes. In retrospect, that's really interesting haha. But at the time, I kept thinking, *"man, I'm putting in a lot of work, why am I only getting a few upvotes?"*

The funny thing is, a rising tide raises all the ships. When my first viral answer hit about 2 months in, (that one got 300k views in one week) that answer helped raise all the upvotes and views on ALL of my other content. **It was basically a snowball effect.** So write consistently because you never know when one of your answers will go viral and help all of your other answers.

INTERVIEW WITH CHARLES TIPS

Former Science Editor, Writer, Venture Entrepreneur, Seadog

Quora Profile (https://www.quora.com/profile/Charles-Tips): Quora Top Writer 2015, Published Writer (Time, Inc., The Huffington Post, Business Insider), Most Viewed Writer in 17 Topics

What got you started with Quora?

I came across a mention of Quora on the Internet a year ago around January 2014. And I'd never heard of it. At first, I thought, "Well, I'll look at it." The first thing that came up was a question about what you've learned about writing.

I've learned a lot about writing because I started out a terrible writer, and now I'm pretty decent. I spent a lot of time learning and I wrote professionally. When I started out, I was absolutely dreadful and I had to bootstrap my way up as a writer.

I thought I might have a lot of good advice, so I answered it. The next thing you know, I'm getting upvotes by the dozen and they're from all over the world and I'm going, **"Damn. This a resource."** I'm getting feedback from people everywhere: India, Africa, South America.

> *"You go anywhere else on the Internet and you make a comment; you'll get one, two, three upvotes on any other forum. But, here I was getting them by the dozens and comments from people who were thirsty for more information and I just felt like, 'Wow.' This is different. This is a real conduit between people all over the world."*

Quora's value is in having good dialogue with people anywhere. On topics that matter to them. That caused me to start exploring, and then I got into all the other topics I've tried to be informative in.

What's been the motivation for sticking around with Quora?

One of the things about Quora is that you get to meet people like Brandon Lee and Ellen Vrana. And by going to the Top Writer conferences, you cement these person-to-person relationships. I've got good friends on Quora that I actually haven't met in any other way but through Quora.

Now I've got a social relationship with some people outside of Quora. I've even had people fly out from California to stay with me or chat with me just because of Quora.

My wife and I are actually going up to Boulder, Colorado, in a week or two because of a connection through Quora to an educational facility there. They want us to come do a talk and meet with their people / give them ideas of increasing their markets.

It definitely opens up the world, but I'm not here trying to cater to it.

One thing I have my questions with Quora about is this policy change where you can't promote other people's work anymore. They have this Quora Digest that they promote your work in, but they're promoting what they want to promote.

I have no way to promote stuff I like anymore. If I've got a question that I've answered that I think is good, but it's buried under a bad question or something that's just not getting attention, I have no way to get it some air, some breathing room. That's very frustrating.

I feel like I'm their writer and they can do with me what they want. What appealed to me in the early days was that it was democratic. I could spot things and promote it and then other people would promote it and next thing you know, somebody's on the radar. A hidden writer could be brought into the spotlight because people were promoting them. That feels like it's missing and that takes out a lot of the sizzle for me.

Did you ever care about getting more upvotes or views?

No. I've never been worried about popularity.

In fact, I kind of catered the opposite sometimes. I'm 66, I have a different point of view. When you're younger, you may want to build traffic and so forth, that's one thing. When you're 66 and hanging up your spurs, then it's just about, "Here's the truth as I know it, take it or leave it."

Is there a certain way you try to structure your answers?

Yes and no. They come to me so fast. I seldom spend too much time on an answer. Once you've been writing professionally for a long time, it's like "read the question," "start writing the answer."

It just comes to you. Sometimes it's very offbeat; sometimes it's not any standard form. I do make an effort sometimes to give an authoritative answer with links and research and support. But in large part, I reject this whole Internet thing of if you haven't substantiated it with links, it's not true.

You can reject answers about my life experiences all you want, that's fine, but it's my life experience and if it rings true with a few people and they're going, "Wow. I didn't think anybody else felt that way," then that's more important to me than a whole bunch of upvotes. A few comments that say, "Damn. I never knew anybody else thought that way." **That's validating to me.**

What were some of the benefits of becoming a Top Writer?

It got me to meet some wonderful people. Most of the writers are introverted and introverts don't put out a lot of work into meeting each other. Sometimes it's kind of painful to go to a Top Writer conference and sit around with other writers and act shy, but it's actually good to put faces to people and it's been one of the fun things of the last couple of years.

INTERVIEW WITH JORDAN PHOENIX

Founder of Uncommon Sense for 21st Century Living, Author of It's All My Fault: How I Messed Up the World, and Why I Need Your Help to Fix It

Quora Profile (https://www.quora.com/profile/Jordan-Phoenix): Quora Top Writer 2014/2015, Published Writer (Inc., Forbes, The Huffington Post), Most Viewed Writer in 2 Topics

Getting Started

When did you get started with Quora?

I believe I started in fall of 2012. I don't remember how I first discovered it. Maybe I saw it and I clicked through a link on Twitter or something. Then slowly you just start reading it and you get … you put the needle in and you're addicted. That's how a Top Writer gets into Quora haha.

What kept you writing on Quora?

It's a pretty unique experience joining Quora. At first, I went there and I was like, "Well, this is really cool. It's almost like the world's biggest camp fire where you can ask questions and they actually have an angle. They will recommend people that could answer that question for you."

If you're saying, "What is it like to be in a NASA space program?" Quora is able to recommend, "Oh, this person's actually an astronaut and knows what it's like."

As someone who went to college and studied civil engineering for a few years, I thought it was amazing. I had graduated and started working for firms in the North East like in New York and New Jersey before realizing, "This is not for me." I wish Quora was around years ago when I was in college so I could actually ask, "What is your day to day experience like? What are some of the pitfalls?"

Because all I hear is the idealistic view of a certain career. The people who are actually going through it can tell you some of the downsides.

It's easy to get an idea of what the Quora culture is like and know whether or not it's really for you. I like to pay it forward and give information to other people. For example, when people say, "What was your major in?" I say, "This is what I wish someone had told me as a freshman."

When I first started on Quora, I had a very unique experience because **the very first answer that I wrote on Quora to this day is still my number one most upvoted and viewed answer.**

That answer still has a quarter million views, I believe, or close to it. I haven't checked in months. It was hovering there with like 5,000 something up votes. I remember thinking, "Oh my goodness." I remember for a few years as a writer, back in my 2009, 2010... I remember the first day that I got 100 views in my blog and I thought that was the most amazing thing in the world.

A quarter million people is bigger than a lot of small cities in the United States. That's how you get hooked. At first, I never topped that first answer. I have probably 200-300 answers but I never topped that first one. Quora is just a really easy tool to use in general.

Finding Your Niche

Did you intentionally start out trying to target any specific topics?

"I think one of the big advantages of Quora is that it's an amazing way for people who want to be writers to find their niche. One of the biggest things that people tell me about is having trouble figuring out what they should actually write about. I say, **"Don't label yourself. Don't worry about that. Just go on Quora. Just read through a lot of answers. See the styles. See what people are doing."**

After that, only answer questions that you feel pulled to. That you feel like you **can't.. not** answer. It how I did it. I said, "These questions are crying out to me. I can totally give someone really good advice on this topic." Otherwise, I wouldn't answer it. Then, once you start doing that, you have 5 answers, 10 answers, and you'll get up to 20, 30 answers. You'll start to notice a recurring theme... **"What is that question that I'm drawn towards? Is there a reason behind that?"**

Slowly, that's how you carve out your niche. Instead of sitting down with a blank piece of paper and saying, "All right, how do I become a writer and not just give up?" See what you're pulled towards - what you're passionate about. Naturally, it will just happen.

Crafting the Perfect Answer

Do you structure your answers in any certain way?

There's a Top Writer on Quora, Oliver Emberton. He is like the Michael Jordan of Quora. I think he has one answer that has over a million views. For a while, he was the most viewed / upvoted answer for a long time in the entire site. He's a developer, designer and a writer. He actually talks about this process of how he will structure an answer.

> *"I think being authentic is the most important thing. Just giving people a real perspective on something.* A lot of times, there's a lot of noise. If people are just being unabashed and giving you just the same response you could find by Googling something, then no one is going to care that much."

Give something that's authentic perspective where you're really sharing a lot of who you really are. Tell a story about something you went through that was really challenging or something that was really inspiring and outside the box. A wild thing that wouldn't normally happen everyday. That's the kind of thing that gets a lot of people to pay attention.

Also, try adding pictures. If you add a photo to your answer, it's way more likely that people will check out your answer.

How Quora Helps Writers

Did Quora help inspire you to write your self-published book?

Yes. I actually wanted to first write my book seven years before I published it. I went through a big phase of asking myself whether or not I should write it. Do I really know what I'm doing? Is anyone going to want to read it and so on. **Quora definitely was one of the main drivers** that made me ask myself, "Why have I not published it yet?" It's obvious that people like the things I'm writing. Over a million people are reading the things I'm putting out. Obviously there's some value that's being created here.

Before the book came out I noticed that at one point the uncommon sense blog that I had on Quora was the **number two most followed blog in the entire site**. I was like, "Wow, this is something that people are really getting behind. A lot of people have positive reactions to it. Let me just keep rolling with it."

Did you ever try to use Quora to get early feedback on content for your book?

Within my book I took some of the concepts from my hard hitting answers that were really popular and merged some of the lessons where it was appropriate. There's one, it's called "The Hypothetical Stranded Islands of Lima."

It just give you this scenario where you're involved with a plane crash with 100 people. There's no food and no water. You're looking everywhere and there's no food, so you have to climb this mountain to try and see if there's food up there. It's your last hope of survival.

Only 20 of you could make it up to the mountain. The other 80 just couldn't make it. This scenario philosophically asks, "All right. Do you now help everyone else get up the mountain or do you say, Ttough luck. I worked hard for what I have.'" Most of the people on Quora certainly were like, "The right thing to do to is help people up the mountain."

Then, I tell them, "The reason why I created this hypothetical question is because 80% of the people of the world live on $2.50 or less a day." Everyone that's reading this... you have food. You have shelter. You have energy and time to probably help people. You're already actually doing the things in real life that we say, in the hypothetical situation, we do. **That actually got a lot of positive and negative feedback from the Quora community.**

Some people were lashing out because they didn't like looking in the mirror and seeing who they really are. People always say, "Yeah, totally. You'd be savage to let people starve at the bottom," but we do that everyday. We do that when we chase material possessions. Instances like these are things that I know I'm definitely putting in the book.

I did actually ask people, "What would you like me to write about?" Some of the ideas that did very well in my Quora blog articles were put into the book as well. One person who reads Quora actually gave me a compliment in an email that said, "I thought that your book was going to rehash a lot of your articles. I thought you would put articles together and say, here's a book, just to sell it." He was like, "I was really impressed that your book was totally different than your articles. I got so much more information. It wasn't exactly what I expected."

What was the experience of becoming a Quora Top Writer?

I didn't think it was that big of a deal when I got it. Partially because I expected, like I knew that I was going to get it based on the fact that my Quora blog was the #2 most followed.

I just could see through amount of likes, upvotes, shares and views I was getting. I could tell that was going to happen. It wasn't like I had my fingers crossed or anything.

I thought it was really funny at first... I actually wasted so much on the internet that someone gave me an award for it. I can't tell if I'm really proud or ashamed that I got that. It's really funny but ... yeah, it was definitely nice.

It was also cool to just get recognition and to be able to say I got an award for writing. Quora's a pretty popular site. It's like top 500 (or even higher than that) in the world for traffic. To be one of the top writers is like an awesome thing in that regard. Going to the meet-ups and meeting other writers has been really cool too.

Do you think becoming a Top Writer helped you get your answers and your book published in major media?

I think that a lot of it just has to do with whether or not you have a specific answer that satisfies what the publisher is looking for at that time.

"I remember one of my published answers was another hypothetical philosophical situation: Imagine there was a country filled with clones of you.

If there was a Wikipedia article about this country, what would be its biggest strengths and weaknesses? What would it be like to live there? The reason why this is a powerful exercise is because it takes into account a lot of your personality traits. For example, it creates an extreme to where you can really understand how the things you're doing are affecting others.

If you have a bad temper, imagine what traffic will be like in this country.

Imagine now if this country had to become a place where everyone just had an amazing life and there were no problems. People got along really well. Then how would each of these clones have to act?"

That's your blueprint of how to be the type of person that gets along with almost everyone. Huffington Post actually reached out to me and said, "Hey, we really like your answer" and published it later.

Having a following on Quora and then on Twitter helped get my book out there. It helped me get the interviews on TV and podcasts at Forbes. It also helped get onto the Amazon best-seller list in the social activist biography category.

It's all connected. **Quora just opens doors for you.** It's silly, I think, because ... You can be the same person saying, "Hey, I have some ideas on how we can possibly alleviate poverty." You get some responses and say, "Hey, I'm talking at Forbes column, it's about how to alleviate poverty." People will think, "Oh, my goodness. Congratulations. Don't forget about the little people."

You're just like, "I'm the same guy talking about the same thing." Why do you only care about this now that it has a label attached to it? That's how society works. You just get used to it. Personally, I give credit to an answers merit more than where it's been published.

But, if that's how you are going to create change in the world... where people need to associate you with success then whatever. I'll play the game, I'll get published in major media like Forbes.

What were some of the other benefits of using Quora?

I've met a lot of amazing people from all over the world. I think that's the biggest benefit of writing, building international community. Some people I've been friends with for years and we've never actually met face to face.

We just know each other through social media which is really interesting because I feel like when you're in school, your social circles are comprised of people that you met just based on things like where you live, what your socioeconomic background happens to be.

Meanwhile, through mediums like Quora, these are people you pick your friends from. People who make you grow and evolve as a person. Social media like Quora surpasses anything where you can just put your values and your interests out there and ideas for anything that you're interested in.

Then people just emerge out of the woodwork. I totally resonate with that. You're awesome and I totally get you and you're like, "Wow, this is so gratifying beyond money or beyond success or anything." It's just like, "Wow, there's people out there who can understand."

It's just that they see the world the same way that I do. It's a really awesome feeling.

Why should other people use Quora?

Yeah, there are a few things. I also think Quora has reached a certain level. This has to do with my theories I talk about in marketing in social media. I call it the "Gold Rush Theory" or "The Wild West Theory" where you have millions of people looking to strike gold. You dig somewhere. You just have to pick the right place. If you get gold, then good for you. Riding the wave and being in the right place at the right time is super important.

In social media, we're always looking for the next Instagram. The next Quora. The next Vine. Make sure you keep an ear to the ground and see what's going to be the next thing. Let's say you find an interesting social media company that just got $10 or $100 million in VC funding. Their goal is to now get as many eyeballs on their site as possible. That's it. That's their only goal.

They're not worried about setting rules. They're not worried about anything other than we just want to bring people back to our site as often as possible. **If you're one of the first people on that and you're giving really valuable content, all of their money and all of their VC funds are going to go to marketing you.** Sometimes, Quora will tell you that they just sent your answer to 17,000 people in the Quora Digest. Do you know how much it would cost to pay for that kind of traffic yourself?

You're tying your success to Quora's success because they really want to take off. You're tying yourself to a rocket ship.

I feel like my Quora blog was one of the first ones. When they started the blog feature, I happened to be one of the first people to get in on that. I was able to take advantage of that and make a name for myself on Quora. I reach over a million people just in Quora with my own writing. No team. No marketing budget.

In the long term, I plan to learn more about design and video animation so I can add more to my answers.

INTERVIEW WITH DUSHKA ZAPATA

Reader. Writer. Communicator. Introvert.

*Quora Profile (https://www.quora.com/profile/Dushka-Zapata):
Published Writer (Inc., The Huffington Post, Thought Catalog), Most
Viewed Writer in 69 Topics*

Do you remember how and when you got started with Quora?

The first time I was ever on Quora was June 30th 2015. That
was about 4 months ago.

Before that, I had heard many people talk about the site.
Friends would mention things they read or learned on Quora.

My boyfriend, specifically, would quote things he saw on the
site, so I knew it existed. My assumption was that it was a
place where very learned experts, such as PhDs in math, or
astronauts, or well known people in tech, went to answer highly
specialized or specific questions.

I knew one day I would get around to checking it out.

A coworker and I were talking about relationships one morning
and he asked "Dushka, are you on Quora?"

"What do you mean?" I said.

"You should write answers on Quora. You have a very unique
take on things".

And when he said it, I just felt rush of excitement. "I can
WRITE on it?"

That was it for me. The first time I was on it was that same afternoon; I wrote my first answer that same evening. I've been hooked ever since.

What aspects of Quora kept you actively writing on the site?

I want to write. Quora is a place to do just that.

I look at questions and think "I've been there. I know what the most delicate thing is. I know what the best thing to say after someone rejects you is. I most certainly know what love is. I know how I feel about my boyfriend sleeping in the same bed with his female friend. I can most definitely answer that."

For me it's about writing.

The reason why I like writing on Quora specifically (rather than on another site or my own blog) is the people that frequent it.

> *"I find it to be a community of critical thinkers, with opinions and a point of view. People are generous with their commentary and incredible in their support of others."*

I like that I can write, but I also really like the site. I deeply appreciate the BNBR rule. I like that you can both be opinionated and nice. I also like how much I learn about people who are not like me. **I think Quora has changed my perception of the world.**

How did you initially decide which topics you wanted to write about?

That's a great question. What I thought initially was not what ended up happening.

I have been working in communications for 20 years, and among other things I teach people how to give presentations and how to talk to press. Many people assume this means "learning how to spin" and I wanted to write about how nothing could be further from the truth. I teach people how to tell things as they really are. That's the expertise I wanted to bring onto Quora: stop skirting the question. Stop "bridging". Everyone knows you are avoiding the issue. Face it instead. Start telling the truth.

"But then what actually happened, and the real way I pick my topics, is questions pull at me."

"The more passionately I feel about a question, the better and more intensely people react to it."

I have answered questions about giving presentations or being a spokesperson, but I also have found other questions to be irresistible. What are some good ways to appear honest? (the word "appear" attracted me like a magnet!) What is the height of confidence? Do people seriously ask other people to go out on dates? If someone asks if you are intelligent, what's the best way to answer without sounding conceited?

I find these and so many other questions so enticing, I'd rather be answering them than doing almost anything else.

Do you feel that over time Quora has actually made you a better writer?

I have wanted to write every since I knew how to write. I had a diary when I was seven.

Most recently, I started writing very short stories in the form of status updates on Facebook. Saying complicated things in a very succinct way felt deeply satisfying. Facebook gave me a platform to practice brevity.

On Quora, I found that when I was succinct my answer would be collapsed. I realized that to be truly useful, to really provide a tool for someone else to apply, I needed to provide more detail; to extend myself. Quora has forced me to exercise a different writing muscle.

On a related note, thanks to the variety of the questions, I feel like I'd never run out of things to write about. It's an intoxicating thing, to feel like I'll always have something to say.

Is there a way that you like to structure your answers?

Well, let me explain something first:

- I tend to think in bullets.

- I am in the habit of breaking things down.

- I find this makes things easier to digest.

- It certainly makes it easier to follow.

This "thought format" is very compatible with Quora.

I also go out of my way to:

- Speak from my own experience

- Provide context with my life as a backdrop

- Explain how I arrived at something that worked for me

- Offer steps that I followed that might help the reader

And finally:

I like to surprise those who follow me consistently with something unexpected. An answer in the format of a poem; or a story told mostly through photos. **I want to give the gift of delight sometimes - go beyond just answering the question.**

Regarding advice, the intent is "I don't know you or your life or your culture, but this is what worked for me". This way I am not meddling with something I know nothing about (such as giving advice with no sense of what another person's life is like) while still providing something that I hope people can relate to and can find useful.

You're one of the few writers we know who does 0 self-promotion in your answers. What was your decision behind that?

Let me start by saying that I am in awe of people who do this well. Linking to other things, inviting people to follow you elsewhere or read your blog, I think is a valuable skill. I constantly read answers that make me want to follow people (to learn more about whatever it is they are doing.)

I myself do not have a long profile. I do not provide links or promote anything. The truth is I don't know how to do so without people feeling like I'm trying to sell them something.

"My intent is: this is what I've learned from my life. If it works for you, awesome. It it doesn't, great. I'm not going to try to convince you or push you. I want you to use it if you find it helpful."

Maybe some day I will learn to do this the right way: where it's perceived as something useful, as an added value, rather than something promotional.

Yet another thing I hope Quora can teach me.

From your writing, have you seen benefits outside of the Quora platform?

I met you. In the same vein, I have had contact with other great writers.

I plan to reach out to some people on Quora whom I have come to really like to suggest a meeting in person, so I know it will be a great networking tool. (The introvert in me keeps putting this off.)

I love that some of my answers have been published on The Huffington Post, Inc. and Thought Catalog. I'm looking forward to seeing more of my work get published. I'm very excited about your book!

I'm curious to see what else Quora brings me. I expect good things come when you put earnest effort into something.

You've been on Quora for a relatively short period of time yet your answers are getting thousands of upvotes and millions of views. You're also a Most Viewed writer in 69 topics. What do you think has led to your success?

Your co-author Imran wrote me a note and said, "I want to know how you managed to have over four million views in the last 30 days."

My answer was "I don't know." That's the truth.

My boyfriend's answer is that I write about things that affect people. Feelings. Rejection. Love. Accepting who you are. (I am "most viewed" across more than 60 categories, and they all relate in some way to experiences and emotions.)

I have not been able to determine or predict which answers will get more upvotes. I once wrote an answer that I super loved (I'm blind. What does it feel like to see?) that did not get a lot of attention (compared to others.)

When I write things about love, or relationships, or how to deal with your inner introvert who wants to stay home when your friends are inviting you to a party, more people seem to read it.

"Dushka," my boyfriend says, "when you write about what it feel like to see, it's poetic but not relatable. When you write about rejection, people feel understood, because they are."

I think my boyfriend might be right. (Whatever you do, don't tell him I said that.)

At the end of the day, what I want is for people to know that there is nothing more powerful than accepting who you are.

On a different but related note I'm very single minded. I'm "all in". I have been (naturally) consistent with my writing, and I think being consistent is another factor in getting, as you put it, "millions of views".

I wonder if one day I'm going to wake up to find my views have dwindled to 8 or 9.

That's when I remind myself that the best part of all of this is the writing.

I'll get to do that no matter what.

What lasting tip would you leave for other writers on Quora?

Check out the site. Find what you like. Explore the questions and see if you feel some of them pull at you. Maybe you are attracted to something entirely different that Quora needs too: editing the questions, for example, or asking really, really good ones (the right question will open any door.) Find something that you find irresistible and do that.

"Be who you are. Be true to your nature. And don't bother writing (or editing, or asking questions) without passion."

INTERVIEW WITH NICOLAS COLE

Writer (www.nicolascole.com), Fitness Model, Entrepreneur, Self Development Coach

Quora Profile (https://www.quora.com/profile/Nicolas-Cole-1): Quora Top Writer 2015, Published Writer (Time, Inc., Fortune, Forbes, The Huffington Post, Business Insider, PopSugar, Thought Catalog, Observer), Most Viewed Writer in 28 Topics

Getting Started

What do you think about the concept of this book?

Awesome. It sounds like an awesome project.

It's actually something that I considered doing a little while ago, just because I 100% agree that Quora is **one of the most underrated social media platforms right now.** I mean I'm the first one to walk around and tell people that over 50 percent of my web traffic comes straight from Quora. A lot of people will message me all the time being like, "Why don't people up vote my stuff more?" Or "Why don't I get as many views?"

I think it's a cool thing all around. I actually would like to share a couple things you touched upon with people, because I feel like I have **cracked the code** with Quora in terms of **how to get your stuff picked up by bigger publications or how to write something that has the ability to get a lot of traction** very quickly.

When I approached it, I was very clear about how I wanted to build a personal brand, so everything that I wrote, every single question that I chose, in some way ... even if they were on completely unrelated industries ... were giving different perspectives on the same personal brand. I think that's a huge thing, too. If you really want to **dominate Quora** or if you want to become a **Top Writer,** if you want to **generate traffic for yourself**, it's really about ... **getting clear on who are you?** What's your personal brand? Then, everything you write has to keep feeding that.

What got you first interested in writing?

I started with Quora a little over a year ago. My background is very, very writing based. When I was in high school and playing World of Warcraft / competing with an elite group of players, they came out with a website called Game Riot. It was a very early version of social media, in a sense, where you could create a profile and anyone could blog. They gamified it where the top five or ten most viewed blogs were featured on the front page. I found out about it when it launched, and I ended up just writing in there frequently because I enjoyed it.

Within a couple of months I was in the top ten most viewed blogs on the site. Within a year, I think I had probably the most popular mage blog on the internet. Even at an early age I just always enjoyed writing online. I figured out how to build a personal voice, a personal brand. I got that. Then, after I stopped playing the game I fell out of writing.

I didn't find anything like that until Quora because I had tried blogs, but the problem is so many people are like, "I want to start a blog," but they have **no idea how to get traffic.**

It's hard because the only reason that I saw success at 17 was because the traffic was already there. It was built into the site like Quora, and if you wrote stuff and you were in early or you wrote controversial stuff, then you got the views and you got featured on the front page. The traffic was already there for you to get. You can't do that with a blog and that's the hardest thing. You have to find other sources of social media traffic like Facebook or Twitter or Instagram to direct back to your blog.

When I started building my Instagram following, I was interested in being an influencer and I knew the power of having an audience. I was really just early in figuring out what that meant for myself. A friend of mine said, "You should look at Quora. As a writer I think you'd really like it." At first I was just a lurker and then I started writing. Within two months **one of my answers went viral** (https://www.quora.com/ Is-it-possible-to-change-your-mentality-such-that-you-cannot-recognize-yourself-anymore). Then... I was hooked.

Do you think your viral answer is what kept you writing on Quora?

To be honest, I would have kept writing regardless, because, like I said, it solved the issue I had which was, I don't know how to find traffic by just creating a blog on Blogspot or Medium. I did see that Quora had people, and with the people came the views, comments, and upvotes.

Quora's gamification is what kept me around, but when that post went viral, and that's still my biggest post ... that **got over a million views** and it **went on the front page of Reddit.** It started everything, to be honest. That showed me the power. The fact that even though you're writing on Quora, there's an **extension that it can give you to other platforms** - that's much harder to do on other social media platforms.

Finding Your Niche

How did you initially pick topics to write about?

Well, what I had originally set out for was the fact that I had already built an audience on Instagram that was fitness based, so I went into it seeing, "OK, there are topics for fitness and bodybuilding and stuff like that."

When that answer went viral, I saw that it was way bigger than that and it was actually more about self-development and the overall fitness / health would play a smaller part of it, but that wasn't the sole focus.

That's when I really started to get a lot more attention. If you look, **self-development is huge** on Quora. There are a lot of niches that you can get into. You can be the expert in nutrition, music, investing or whatever.

> *"Overall, I think the reason people go to Quora is that it all comes down to wanting to develop some part of themselves. Something to do with self-improvement."*

Did you try to specifically target questions that might go viral within topics?

Well, on the surface, you can tell **which questions are shortsighted and which are a lot bigger** based on the tone of the question. Some people will just ask, "How do I get better at doing this" about one thing, versus someone who's saying, "How can I improve my life in general?"

It's funny, I was always really into debate in high school. What I realized is that the people who are really successful on Quora

(James Altucher comes to mind here), **don't go into it saying, "I'm just going to answer this question."**

"What they do is **take that question as a prompt card** *and then they basically walk into it saying,* **"OK, I'll address your question somewhere in my answer, but I'm going to use this to creatively say whatever I want."***

I started to realize that it was more about **creative writing, telling stories, and sharing personal experiences.** *The question is just the starting point. It's not like anyone can answer the question and be done.*

It's whoever can take the question, run with it, and really get you to think about something that you probably didn't even know you wanted to know about in the first place."

Crafting Your Answers

Do you find that there's an optimal way to structure your answers on Quora?

Yeah, format is huge; people really like small sections. You know from BuzzFeed that **people really like lists.** I know that if someone asks, "How can I improve my life," if I write them an essay it has to be really well written to keep them engaged the entire time.

"If I say, "OK, that's a big question so let me give you ten things that you can do to improve your life," then I write one thing, a title, bold that and then underneath it maybe give a paragraph of what that means. Then, go to two. Bold that, and write another paragraph of what that means.

That's a lot easier to digest and I find that's what gets you traction quicker. *At the same time, if you are going to write a long answer, it always helps if you include a **personal story because the personal stories are what people relate to,** and ultimately, **when they're asking that question they're asking it not from a logical place, but from an emotional place.***

They want to know that they're not alone or they want to know that someone else has experienced that, too, and everyone is just trying to share their wisdom. It's very much a marketing approach.

People aren't going to remember what you told them, but they'll remember how you made them feel. *Think about all the answers on Quora that have kept your attention. They're all personal stories. Every single one."*

Even if it's someone explaining, "Here's how to structure your company," somewhere in their answer they'll say, "When I was 32, I went broke because I was trying to structure my first company and here's how I learned all the hard lessons." That's a personal story.

What metric do you try to focus on for your answers?

I care most about views. I think with other platforms, it's all about followers, but I've noticed that my followers go up consistently anyway, so there's no reason to worry about it.

I also know that it's harder to get followers on Quora just because it's not as big as a Facebook or Twitter. I think that my primary metric is views because at the end of the day, if I say I have 5,000 followers on Quora most people are like, "Cool. What's Quora?" If I say, "I have 5 million views on Quora," people are like, **"I've never heard of that but how can I figure it out?"**

Cracking the Code to Getting Published

Can you walk us through what you mean by "cracking the code" of getting picked up by major publications?

Basically, how it works, is that Quora has relationships with all of the big magazines: Time Inc., Forbes, Huffington Post, all of them. Every Friday, Quora has editors who pitch stories to the people they have the connections with at each of these publications.

For myself, I didn't even know how my first answer got picked up to be published until someone messaged me and was like, "Hey, we wanted to use your article on Inc." I was like, "Oh, cool. I didn't even know Quora did this."

Eventually, you start to know who those people are on Quora and so in my message inbox, I have five or six people I know that are always looking for content and are pitching content on Fridays. Whenever I write something that I think would be a good fit, I immediately send them a private message and I say, "Hey, I thought this might be a good fit for Business Insider or Time." Send them a link and then they go, "Oh, OK. Cool. We'll pitch it."

It's just a more direct funnel. Then, on top of that, I did more research into what sorts of answers these publications pick up. Unfortunately, they're probably not going to pick up a long-winded essay unless you're a celebrity that's just going to get read because you're a celebrity.

"The things that they will pick up from lesser-known people like myself are very concise **where you're either teaching or the answer has something to do with self-development / self-improvement**. It also tends to be in a **digestible form, like a list.**"

If I look back at all the stuff I've gotten picked up in the past three months, it's all been "Seven Ways to ..." "Ten Ways to ..." "Five Ways to ..." If I see those questions that are very open and very broad, i.e., "How can I simplify my life?" - then great. That's super broad and I can do whatever I want with that.

I go in and I say, "OK, well here's seven ways you can improve your life," and then I make it very easy for the intended audience to digest but still have depth. I'll think to myself, is this the type of thing that someone who reads Inc. or Huffington Post would read? Keeping that person in mind, I'll write it and immediately send the link to an editor. I'd say, 90% of the time, I'll usually get a piece picked up once a week.

What are some interesting hacks you've done with these published answers?

The thing that I've only recently realized is that whenever one of your answers gets picked up by Inc. or other media publications, they don't spell check it. They copy and paste. I'm reading my Inc. article and there's even spelling errors and I'm like, "Great." It encourages you to treat every answer as professionally as you can, which is good. At the same time, I didn't realize that because they copy/paste, what also happens is if **you put your blog address in the answer you now have a massive publication pointing to your website.** It's amazing.

I didn't really put that together until pretty recently, and so now it's like, "OK, I can't be too overt about promoting my own stuff but if I can, I'll sneak a web link somewhere in the body, not in the signature." That way, whenever that answer gets reposted on Inc. or Huffington Post, I get that extra SEO advantage for my website.

Additionally, if people are reading your reposted answer they might go, "Oh, cool. Let me check this out," and go to your website.

The Top Writer Experience

What was your experience of becoming a Top Writer?

It was awesome, actually. For example, I think they give the top-writer badge to something like the top one percent of writers. When I played World of Warcraft, the title that I'd always wanted was "Gladiator" and they gave that to the top 0.5 percent.

In a sense when I got Top Writer status, I felt like I had hit Gladiator again, which was really cool. I'm really big into gamification stuff and I love the concept. The thing that was so interesting to me was that before I got it, there was a two-month period where I was very popular on the site and I was getting a lot of traction.

There were a lot of people commenting saying, "Why isn't this person a Top Writer yet?" It was sort of the fact that I wasn't a Top Writer that I think actually made people more interested, because it's like being an underdog. As soon as I became a Top Writer, I noticed this two-month lapse where I felt like my traction went down significantly because people went to my profile and were like, "Oh, another Top Writer. Whatever."

I think there was something to that underdog status, which was really cool, but now I feel like I've moved to a different goal ... I think there's a transition period and now I'm just trying to catch up to James Altucher. That's my goal.

> *"To be honest, the thing that was the coolest was the fact that at the same time that they told me that they were going to give me Top Writer status, the thing that made me more happy was that they actually chose one of my answers to put in their* **2014 Anthology.**
>
> *I didn't even know this anthology existed.* **You realize I went to college for writing. My dream is to be a writer. I want to write books. The hardest thing and the thing that they told us all the time in**

school was you have to prove that you are worth publishing."

It's funny because now I feel like I wouldn't even go to a big publishing house. I would just publish independently anyway. If you're going to get picked up by a publishing house, they want to see that someone else has validated your work.

What really struck me is that Quora is basically a social media platform for writers, and through Quora, I now have a published piece of work in a book that I can point to. On top of that, my published work is actually on the topic of my own self-published book that I'm currently writing about. There is no better validation than that right there.

When they told me I was a Top Writer, I didn't even care. **But when I got that Anthology book in the mail, I mean, dude, it was the coolest thing to see your work in a printed book.**

The other cool thing about being a Top Writer are the in-person meetups. I plan on going to one in December here in New York, which will be my first one. Who else is doing stuff like this?

"Quora might not have as many users as Twitter or Facebook. But think about it, **they're taking something that's online and they're bringing it out to the world.** *They're saying,* **"OK, now you have a piece in a published book,"** *or* **"You have the ability to go meet these people online in real life."** **You're all part of this community together and you can all network together.** *That is irreplaceable. That is truly amazing."*

Final Thoughts

Have you noticed any other tangible benefits from writing on Quora?

Yeah, absolutely. After that first answer went viral, that's what basically gave me the validation to create my own website and to also put the eBook series up that I have, which is just focused on working out. What are my routines? How do I eat? I just made what people were asking me for. That's just the beginning.

I plan on putting a lot more up there but that was the starting point. I wanted to see if it worked instead of giving it away for free, I charged people for it. **I now have data that shows a direct correlation between how much I write on Quora in a month and how much revenue I bring in.**

There's a very clear correlation in writing every day, especially in the fitness sections on Quora and bringing in "X" amount of revenue. If I write more in another category or if I don't write as much altogether, direct correlation. Revenue goes down.

One thing I noticed from another Top Writer, Oliver Emberton, was that at the bottom of his answers he would put a signature to his blog and I started doing that. This led to better conversions. That's something that I've been testing off and on.

Any last tips for other writers or people just getting started on Quora?

I would just say **it's the habit.** In the six months before I hit Top Writer, **I wrote every single day.** Every single day I wrote at least one answer. If you do that you're going to win just by numbers. The sheer volume of content you're putting out, something is going to hook. If you're writing really good content, and you're doing that every day, you're going to do well. I would really drill into people that you can't expect to be popular by writing once a week.

Can you tell our readers about the book that you're self-publishing?

Basically, the memoir that I've been working on for a while now, hoping to finish soon, is called "Confessions of a Teenage Gamer." It's going to be a retelling, in a sense, of what it's like to come of age, be a teenager, and be a hundred percent absorbed in competitive gaming.

It's as much funny and reminiscent of what adolescence is like, but at the same time, talks about what it's also like to be one of the highest-ranked players in North America and show up to school and have no one know it. What it's like to be going on two hours of sleep and trying to compete and trying to get a sponsor. Sneaking around your parents at night because you're not allowed to stay up late.

All us gamers have ridiculous stories. To be honest, I'm hoping that by sharing all of the ridiculous things that happened, other gamers will come out and be like, "You know what? That's exactly what I did, too." I think because everybody I talk to about it, they're like, "Yeah, you know what? I do remember that. That was a good time in my life. It was fun." A lot of us can relate to it.

You can sign up for the release here:
http://www.nicolascole.com/confessions-of-a-teenage-gamer

Closing
Thoughts

By now you should have some really great insights into how powerful a platform Quora can be and should be eager to get started.

Before you do, consider this:

One of the great challenges in life is staying consistent with any journey you undertake to finally see the fruits of your labour.

Quora will challenge you in that.

Many answers you produce when you first start writing will fail to get traction and it'll be very easy to call it quits too early.

Don't. There is gold at the end of the rainbow.

The common theme across all writers who have obtained Top Writer status is one thing:

Consistency

Waking up everyday to answer 1 or 2 questions to hone your writing skills and build up that momentum where people see you regularly posting.

Slowly but surely you'll build up connections, followers and people will start recognizing you for your writing style. It happens quicker than you think but slower than you may want.

And along the way, you'll really help people, make lasting connections grafted with the written word and come to appreciate Quora as more than just another social network but a place where two anonymous individuals can truly connect.

Your friends in writing,

Imran Esmail + Kevin Lee

http://www.quoradomination.com

Made in the USA
Middletown, DE
12 July 2022

69137496R00070